Rethinking Change Management with Nudges:

Transforming Organizations in 45 Minutes

MATT D.M. WATSON, Ph.D.

DEDICATION

To my daughters, Mia and Josie. Since birth, you've both inspired a constant state of change for me. A change into the person I would have never become without you two.

CONTENTS

ACKNOWLEDGMENTS

A special thank you to my wife, Jacquie, who always nudges me to enjoy the present.

CHAPTER 1
DAIMLER CHRYSLER CHANGE
MANAGEMENT EXPERIENCE

"If horses had controlled investment decisions, there would have been no auto industry."

Warren Buffett

Walter Chrysler formed the Chrysler Corporation in 1925. He led the company to become one of Detroit's Big Three automakers. For that reason, he is one of the founding fathers of the early automobile.

Gottlieb Daimler was one of the first pioneers of the internal combustible engine. He took that idea to market and began a car company in the 1890s. In 1926, the Daimler company merged with Benz. As a result, Daimler-Benz became the main German automaker and noted luxury car throughout the twentieth century.

In May of 1998, Chrysler and Daimler-Benz merged to become DaimlerChrysler AG. The merger was intended to create a new giant automaker that could stretch across Europe and the Americas. With projected annual sales of over $150 billion, the company was poised to be the dominant automaker. This combination would address the full consumer auto market while capitalizing on economies of scale by maximizing German efficiency and American innovation[1].

The merger had a tough beginning fraught with significant cultural differences. Chrysler had a reputation as an agile, action-oriented company with a

[1] M. Watkins, "Why Daimler Chrysler Never Got Into Gear," *Harvard Business Review*, 2007.

flat management hierarchy. Daimler, however, was renowned for being methodical, analytical, and utilizing a vertically organized management structure.[2] Compounding these differences was the fact that the merger was soon revealed to be a takeover. Chrysler did not have a board seat in the new corporation and had reduced influence over how the two companies would become one.[3] The push was to adopt Daimler's management, standard operations, and culture instead of creating a new work model together.[4]

Over the following years, organizational disaster ensued, accompanied by management misalignment. Leadership infighting became the norm. The bickering led to multiple reorganizations and layoffs, which, in turn, led to industry-declared poor vehicle designs and lagging manufacturing practices.[5] Eventually, the board decided to run the companies as separate entities so as to not degrade the brands.

---

[2] N. Beotra, "Daimler-Chrysler (DCX) Merger: A Cultural Mismatch," 16 October 2016. [Online]. Available: https://medium.com/@beotra.nehaa/daimler-chrysler-dcx-merger-a-cultural-mismatch-2cbb3a05321d.
[3] R. D. Lewis, "Cross-cultural issues relating to the Daimler Chrysler Merge - Case Study," 27 April 2016. [Online]. Available: https://www.crossculture.com/cross-cultural-issues-at-the-daimlerchrysler-merge-case-study/.
[4] C. a. H. Stadler, "Shell, Siemens, and Daimler Chrysler: Leading Change in Companies with Strong Values," *Long Range Planning*, pp. 1-37, 2005.
[5] A. a. S. J. D. Cohen, "Daimler Chrysler Merger: The Quest to Create 'One Company'," *Babson College*, pp. 1-26, 2004.

By 2007, the gas crisis had swung into full effect, and Chrysler could not survive. Given a prime excuse, Daimler sold Chrysler to Cerberus Capital Management to bring it back to life. This allowed Daimler to wash its hands of one of the greatest change management failures.

On a massive scale, this takeover demonstrates the same behaviors of many change management failures: ignoring environmental differences, not engaging with stakeholders who will be impacted, and forcing behavioral changes upon an embedded organizational culture. While this was a takeover, the execution of Daimler's change management was an abject disaster for both parties.

Automobile U.S. Market Share

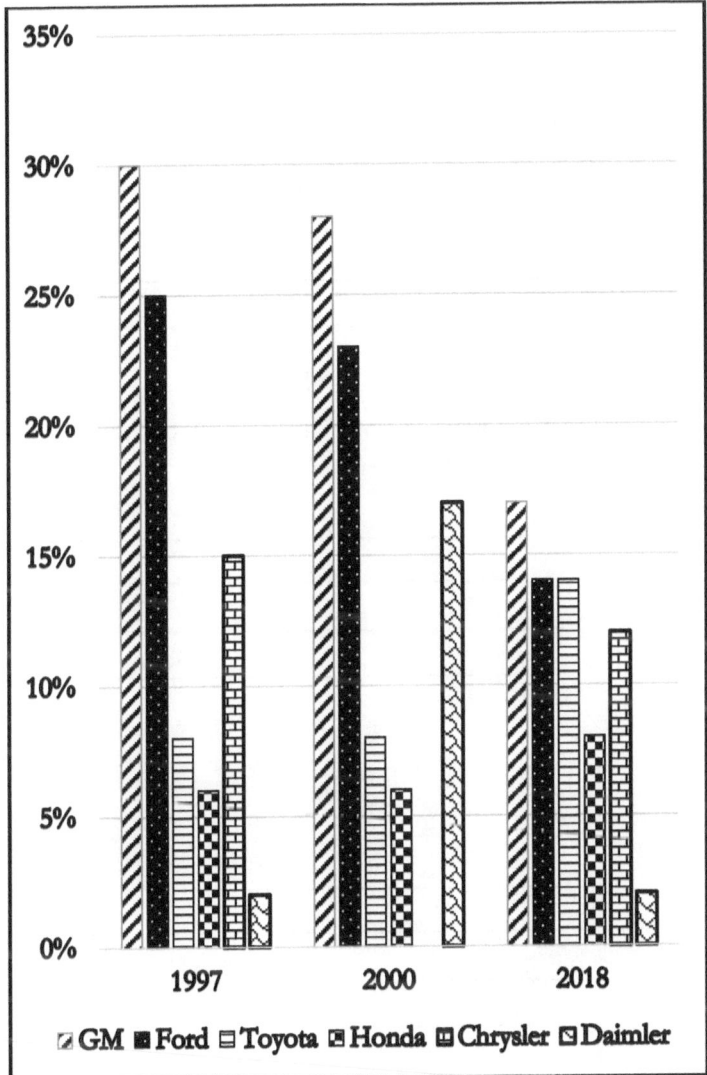

NOTES:

1. What was a change you experienced that
    ended up in disaster?

    _____

    _____

    _____

    _____

2. What were the outcomes of the event?

    _____

    _____

    _____

    _____

3. Why did it fail?

    _____

    _____

    _____

    _____

CHAPTER 2
HISTORY OF CHANGE
MANAGEMENT

"People are usually afraid of change because they fear the unknown. But the single greatest constant of history is that everything changes."

Yuval Noah Harari

The roots of change management stretch back to World War II and the mass mobilization of soldiers. This led to the study of management and, later, the effects of change. In 1948, Lester Coach and John French studied the motivational issues centered around change initiatives, identifying behavioral resistance. Their work defined the three types of change: planned, continuous, and transitional.

In the 1950s, Kurt Lewin developed one of the first change models. The model consisted of three stages: unfreeze, change, and refreeze. In 1969, Elizabeth Kubler-Ross published her five stages of grief and pointed to the correlation that was mirrored by individuals experiencing the death of a loved one and the employees during the change management process.[6]

With the 1990s came the advancement of globalization. General Electric was able to leverage successful change approaches taking advantage of a slower transitioning market. Its approach was so successful that it was able to turn it into a new consulting business.[7]

---

[6] W. W. Burke, Organizational Change: Theory and Practice, New York: Sage, 2002.
[7] S. Levine, "What can we learn from the history of change management?," 18 April 2016. [Online]. Available: https://www.cuinsight.com/can-learn-history-change-management.html.

With eighty years of practice, organizations continue to struggle with implementing change. Change theorist John Kotter projects that 70% of all change efforts fail because they created environments of decreased morale, missed opportunities, and wasted resources. In retrospect, studies found that the model of reengineering the organization boom of the 1980s ignored people. The model actually made things worse. As practice and models have adjusted, leaders now know the change tools and theory[8] but are failing to apply these tools or involve employees in the change process. This practice has led to poor communication channels,[9] not rewarding quick wins or change successes, making it harder to change ingrained behaviors.

---

[8] B. Syed, "The Evolution of Organizational Change Management," 25 November 2015. [Online]. Available: https://www.linkedin.com/pulse/evolution-change-management-burhan-syed-pmp/.

[9] R. a. F. W. Suddaby, "History and Organizational Change," *Journal of Management,* pp. 19-37, 2017.

History of Change

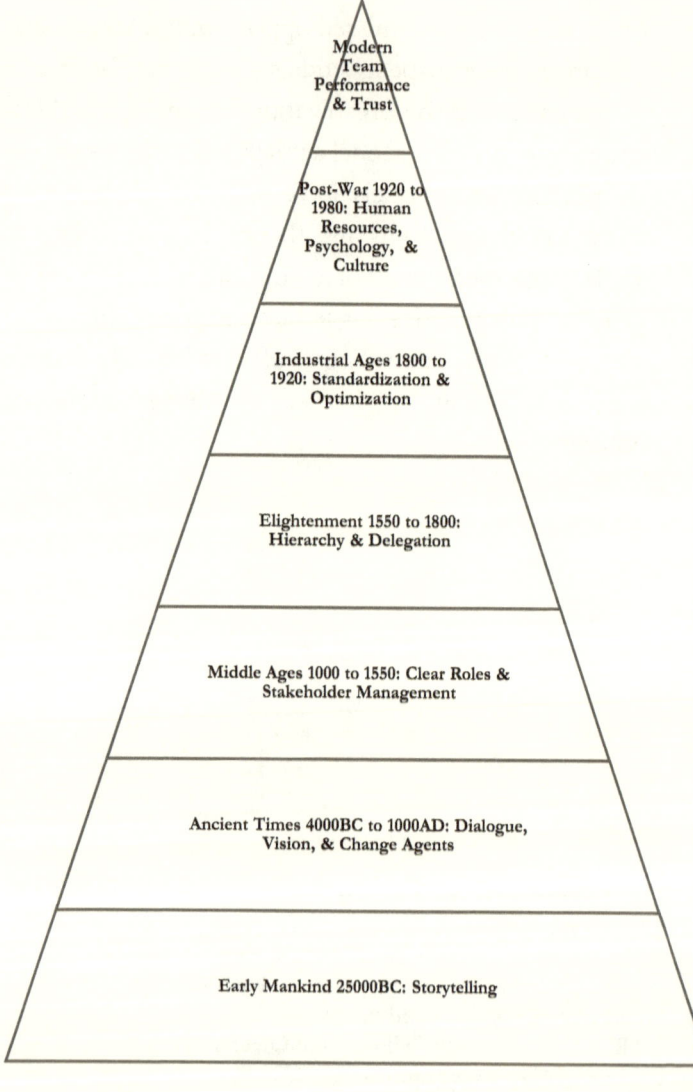

Modern Team Performance & Trust

Post-War 1920 to 1980: Human Resources, Psychology, & Culture

Industrial Ages 1800 to 1920: Standardization & Optimization

Elightenment 1550 to 1800: Hierarchy & Delegation

Middle Ages 1000 to 1550: Clear Roles & Stakeholder Management

Ancient Times 4000BC to 1000AD: Dialogue, Vision, & Change Agents

Early Mankind 25000BC: Storytelling

NOTES:

1. What change models have you experienced?

   _____

   _____

   _____

   _____

2. What roles have you played in change events?

   _____

   _____

   _____

   _____

3. What impact will change management play in your industry over the next 5 years?

   _____

   _____

   _____

   _____

CHAPTER 3
LEWIN'S CHANGE MODEL

"If you want truly to understand something, try to change it."

Kurt Lewin

Kurt Lewin was an early organizational and leadership theorist known mostly for his work on behavioral change. His seminal work identified the formula stating that behavior is a function of the person in the environment.

$$B = f(P, E)$$

His work also initiated discussions on the change process, which he referred to as the three-step model. The model consisted of an organization unfreezing, changing, and refreezing. Later in his life, this model led to his research on analyzing change, which he called a force field analysis. This consisted of analyzing the restraining or driving forces that affect transitions, assessing which are critical, and taking mitigating and maximizing steps on those critical factors.[10]

The Lewin change model focuses on the three stages of how an organization evolves. First, the present state of stable equilibrium is altered or unfrozen. Second, the change introduces new responses to stimuli. Third, the change effort is stabilized and refrozen within the organization.[11]

---

[10] C. Brisson-Banks, "Managing Change and Transitions: A Comparison of Different Models and Their Commonalities," *Emerald insights,* pp. 241-252, 2009.
[11] K. Lewin, Field Theory in Social Science, New York, NY: Harper and Row, 1951.

This revolution was the spark that led to an entirely new field of study. The model was well-received because it was easy to understand conceptually and to apply in practice. Additionally, the model forces the change agent to think past the quantitative side of change management to incorporate the qualitative side. However, the main detractor from this change approach is that it is rudimentary in nature and does not address how to deal with detractors that can derail change efforts.

Lewin's Change Model

Unfreeze
- Determine what needs to change
- Ensure strong leadership support
- Create the need for change
- Manage and understand the doubts and concerns

Change
- Communicate often
- Dispel rumors
- Empower actions
- Involve people in the process

Freeze
- Anchor the changes in the culture
- Develop ways to sustain the change
- Provide support and training
- Celebrate sucesses

NOTES:

1. Have you observed the Lewin Freeze Model in action?

   _____

   _____

   _____

   _____

2. What did you like about the Freeze Model?

   _____

   _____

   _____

   _____

3. What would you change in the Freeze Model?

   _____

   _____

   _____

   _____

CHAPTER 4
KOTTER'S CHANGE MODEL

"Nothing undermines change more than behavior by important individuals that is inconsistent with verbal communication"

John P. Kotter

Harvard Business School professor John Kotter published his seminal work, "Leading Change," in 1995, which codified the Kotter change model. He created an approach that could handle greater complexity than Lewin's change model and address change resistance. Kotter designed his model as an eight-step process, consisting of step-by-step instructions on how to implement change.

The process starts with creating a sense of urgency to spark the movement. The goal is to form a powerful coalition to build political support. Next, one must create a vision to establish a clear goal and then communicate the vision to align the organization. Following this, the organization must remove obstacles to empower the change and create short-term wins to build momentum. Lastly, leaders must sustain acceleration to demonstrate the success of the change, and institute the change so that it becomes part of the culture.[12]

The introduction of Kotter's change model represented a new era of change management. It created an opportunity to engage hard-to-sway employees by using a coalition-based team that influences formal and informal leaders to enact the change. Lastly, it provides the user with a robust

[12] J. P. Kotter, Leading change, Boston, MA: Harvard Business School Press, 1996.

checklist that any manager can apply.

Conversely, the Kotter model is a top-down model. The model fails to engage all levels of the organization that are impacted by the change. It can also be used as a fear-based model by attempting to create a sense of urgency. In addition, the process gives the impression of being mechanical and robotic rather than authentic.

Kotter's Change Model

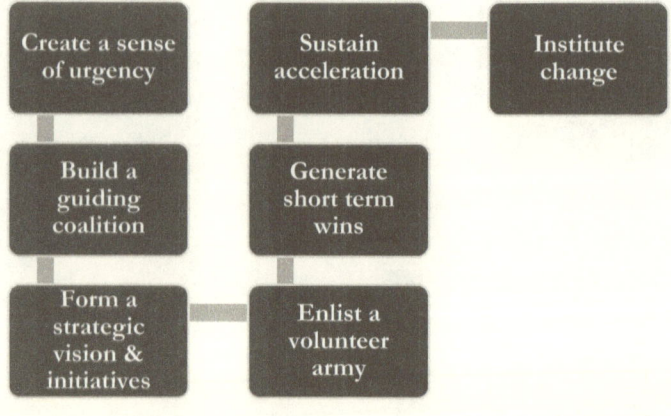

NOTES:

1. Have you observed the Kotter Change Model in action?

   _____
   _____
   _____
   _____

2. What did you like about Kotter's Model?

   _____
   _____
   _____
   _____

3. What would you change in Kotter's Model?

   _____
   _____
   _____
   _____

CHAPTER 5
HIATT'S ADKAR CHANGE MODEL

"If the facts don't fit the theory, change the facts."

Albert Einstein

I n 1998, Jeff Hiatt developed a practical change tool that focused on the people element of change. Most noteworthy, the model was intended to be a coaching and mentoring tool. It was meant to help employees through the change process and determine if activities had the desired response.[13] The overarching belief was that change begins at the personal level. As a result, the ADKAR model was created as a bottom-up change management model.[14]

The ADKAR model is based on five key phases that the employee transverses with the first being the awareness of the need for change. The second phase is to understand people's desire to participate and support the change. The third phase focuses on the team's ability to gather knowledge of the change event and their subsequent ability to learn new skills while managing behavior. The final phase is to reinforce and sustain the change.[15]

The ADKAR change model has numerous

---

[13] "ADKAR Change Management: creating change in Individuals," 6 November 2018. [Online]. Available: https://www.educational-business-articles.com/adkar-change-management/.
[14] "Organizational Change Models and Their Applications," 6 November 2018. [Online]. Available: https://communicationmgmt.usc.edu/blog/3-organizational-change-models-and-their-applications/.
[15] "What is the ADKAR Model," 6 November 2018. [Online]. Available: https://www.prosci.com/adkar/adkar-model.

positives. It focuses on leaders helping employees understand, interact with, and carry out changes. The model directs attention to goal accomplishment, and it can be adaptable to any corporate structure. On the negative side, the ADKAR model struggles with managing highly complex changes; the model is built for incremental changes with a narrow focus.

Hiatt's ADKAR Change Model

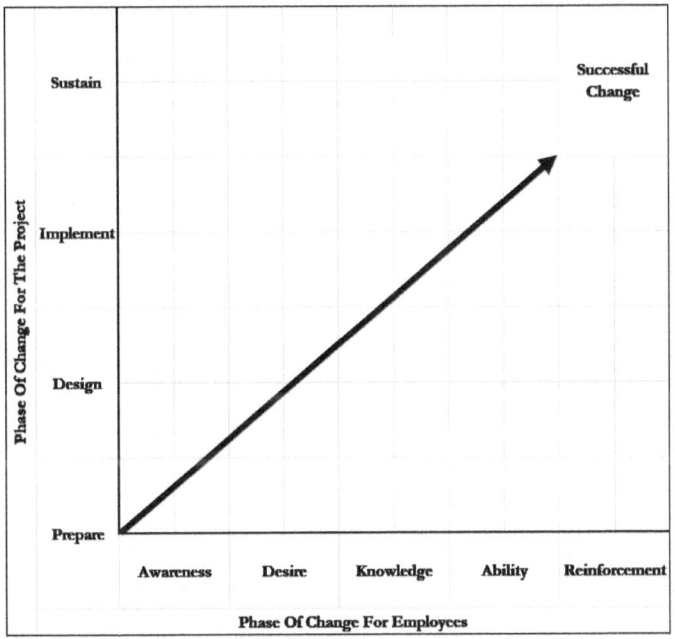

NOTES:

1. Have you observed the ADKAR Model in action?

    _____

    _____

    _____

    _____

2. What did you like about the ADKAR Model?

    _____

    _____

    _____

    _____

3. What would you change in the ADKAR Model?

    _____

    _____

    _____

    _____

CHAPTER 5
NUDGE THEORY CHANGE MODEL

"The best way to predict the future is to invent it."

Alan Kay

Developed by Richard Thaler and Cass Sunstein, nudge theory was popularized in their self-named book, capitalizing on Thaler's Nobel prize–winning work in economics. The theory focuses on how our brains have built-in cognitive biases that prevent us from making the right decisions. For example, numerous people continue to drink soft drinks, knowing full well that they are bad for them.[16]

Humans display systematic deviations from 100% rational decision-making. These deviations prevent a person from making decisions that are in their best interest. Because of these hardwired biases, it is difficult to make rational decisions. Looking closer at the *why* of human behavior, it becomes clear that environments influence people's choices. Thaler's nudging theory is based on influencing people's decisions by influencing their environments.[17]

While there are many variations of nudge theory in policymaking and social science, the philosophy also aligns closely with change

---

[16] S. a. G. O. Ledbetter, "The Nagging Issues of Nudging," 6 November 2018. [Online]. Available: https://medium.com/practical-motivation-science/the-nagging-issues-of-nudging-f0af3a8f8b5.
[17] R. H. &. S. C. R. Thaler, Nudge: Improving decisions about health, wealth, and happiness, New Haven, CN: Yale University Press, 2008.

management. Offered in a step-by-step approach that resembles Kotter's change model, the nudge change model begins by clearly defining the change. The change agent considers the change from the employees' point of view and uses evidence to show the employees the best option. Next, the change agent presents the change as a choice and to listen to feedback. Lastly, the change agent limits obstacles and keeps the momentum going by delivering short-term wins.

Nudge theory has numerous positives as its intent is to place people in positive environments and people-centric cultures. It has empirically demonstrated its effectiveness at inducing behavioral changes and incorporates autonomy and individual decisions. Conversely, it can also come across as manipulation to the team, especially if used inappropriately. In addition, it highlights the question of whether the change is ideal for the individual or for the organization.

<u>Nudge Change Model</u>

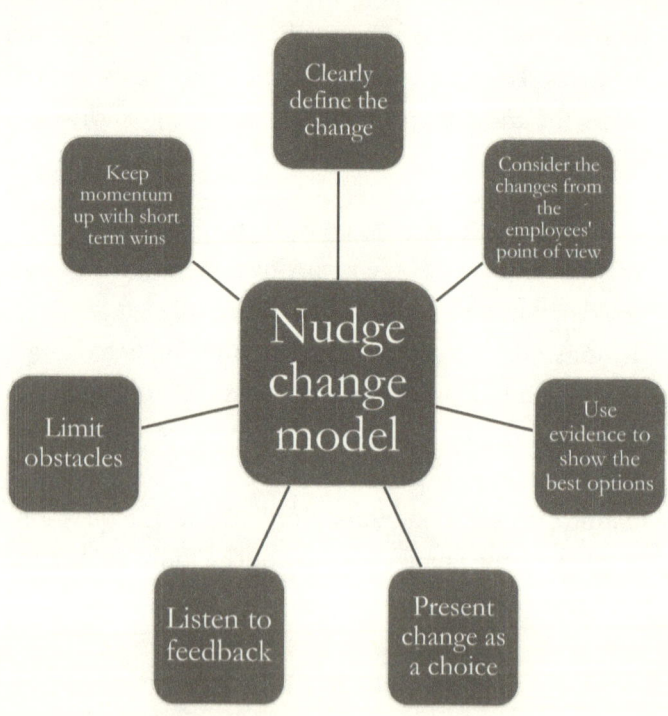

NOTES:

1. Do you have an example of where you have been nudged to act?

   _____

   _____

   _____

   _____

2. How could you apply nudges into an upcoming change?

   _____

   _____

   _____

   _____

3. How do you separate nudging someone into behavior without manipulating them into something not in their best interests?

   _____

   _____

   _____

   _____

CHAPTER 7
9X ORGANIZATIONAL CHANGE MANAGEMENT (OCM) APPROACH

"The world hates change, yet it is the only thing that has brought progress."

Charles Kettering

The 9x organizational change management approach combines the positive attributes of each of the previously mentioned change theories. Like Lewin's "Freeze Model," this approach goes beyond the quantitative aspects to focus on the people impacted by the change. The approach resembles Kotter's model, incorporating a checklist approach and addressing change detractors. Linked with the ADKAR model, it uses bottom-up planning to engage those affected by the change. Lastly, it adopts the nudge theory's choice architecture practice to influence positive behaviors to enact the change.

Beginning with leadership alignment, the goal of the change manager is to ensure that there are a clear vision and strategy in place that everyone in leadership can understand, discuss, and support. This also helps guide the team in defining what success looks like. This definition can range from project completion to a complete culture change.

Associated with the change's vision and measurable success is an understanding of its importance to the organization and the urgency behind it. Importance and urgency play an interconnected role in terms of behavioral change. For example, a doctor can tell a patient during numerous physical exams that they need to eat healthier and to quit smoking with no corrective actions taken. Yet, if this advice comes after a heart attack, which is an important and urgent event, the patient is more likely to adopt the behavioral change.

As the leadership team achieves alignment, the next step is to review the event milestones. This will help identify flashpoints that may occur. Each change has a catalyst event that causes disruption. Being able to understand these at a granular level will allow you to predict the reactions by those affected. For example, imagine that an organization facing a financial crisis must conduct a workforce reduction to stay in business. That event will cause changes throughout the entire workforce, with people being either laid off or forced to incorporate a new working model with fewer people to support ongoing operations.

With a timeline of future events, a change leader can identify the flashpoints where major and minor issues will occur. A stakeholder impact analysis will focus on those spots in order to develop an empathetic understanding of what the issues will be. After an understanding of the issues is developed during the hazard analysis, mitigation plans can be developed to lessen the impact the change will have on the affected. This is the creation of the change roadmap, where the change leader can incorporate various change strategies or mitigation actions into the timeline. This is also the point where choice architecture is applied to the timeline and to the decisions the workforce will be nudged toward.

With the timeline mapped out, communication planning begins with the identification of the timing for the key messages, their content, and their medium. All change plans will have a change announcement. Good change plans will have multiple messages, and a great change plan will have multiple feedback sessions incorporated into the process. During communication planning, the key to adoption and acceptance is to have carefully structured messages that are highly intentional. These are not end-of-the-day messages that are typical tasks, but messages that will be analyzed and dissected. The most important action a manager can take during a change event is to present a clear and concise message that expresses authentic empathy.

During the planned feedback sessions, this is the opportunity to engage the entire organization. Ideally, the facilitator presents the goal of the change while the workforce decides how to make the change happen. This step provides the most risk regarding the success or failure of the change event. It also provides engagement and change acceptance.

As Peter Senge stated, "People don't resist change, they resist being changed." During these sessions, numerous actions will be identified and developed to help make this change successful. The role of the change facilitator is to capture all of these items and build the change action plan. This action plan will then become the living document and reference for moving forward. It should also include a section on quick wins of actions to drive momentum and feedback loops.

9X OCM Change Model

Establish Leadership

Vision & Strategy
Importance & Urgency
Alignment

Road Map

Project Milestones
Flashpoints

Stakeholders

Impact Analysis
Risk Mitigation Strategies

Communications

Message & Medium Planning
Change Announcement

Feedback

Stakeholder Feedback Sessions
Transition Planning Sessions

Execution

Quick Wins
Obstacle Elimination
Finalize Change Plan

NOTES:

1. What is an upcoming change your organization will be implementing?

   _____

   _____

   _____

   _____

2. What key objectives will you put on the change roadmap?

   _____

   _____

   _____

   _____

3. Who will be impacted and how will they react?

   _____

   _____

   _____

   _____

CHAPTER 8
CHANGE TEAM

"It's only after you've stepped out of your comfort zone that you begin to change, grow, and transform"

Roy T. Bennett

Being a competent leader in change management helps the process. However, the use of a specialized team to focus on change execution increases the odds of the initiative being successful. Essential to the 9x approach is the application of four distinct roles. These can be performed by one person, or each role can have a team. The first role is the **change manager** who will be the lead and point person for all things change related.

The change initiator or change owner will be the organizational head of the change effort. The change manager will be the face of the initiative to the workforce. They will be the interface between the leadership team, the change team, and the rest of the organization, while also being the project manager for the entire event. This provides a central source for the change that aligns the organization with one truth and ensuring that each step in the change approach is expertly followed.

Next on the team is the **communications and marketing lead**. This is the individual who carefully crafts each change message. These messages must be consistent and authentic. They are disseminated to ensure that the organization understands why the change is happening, who is affected, and what impacts it will have. The communications and marketing lead also determine how to market the change to the organization with the goal of helping the organization understand the necessity of the change.

Pertinent to the 9x change approach is the heavy influence of change planning developed by those affected by the change. Their role in this process is to provide guidance as an unbiased **facilitator**. The facilitator's role is to reinforce the change message. They also play therapist, letting the affected vent their frustrations over the unsettling news through discussions and workshops. In addition, the facilitator also guides the workforce, moving the team forward and empowering them as to how they will implement the change. Ultimately, the team will decide what their new lives will look like. These facilitated sessions will then produce an ample number of actions to move the change forward, which will then be fed into the change leader's comprehensive project plan.

The last role is a unique role: the **choice architect**. The 9x change approach is the interweaving of nudge theory to help influence the change. Change events are successful once those who are affected subconsciously agree with the change and start to support the movement. This approach calls for engaging the organization, with the goal of helping plan and drive the change by being an active participant in the event. This also cedes control to the organization to decide key aspects of the change. The role of the choice architect is to identify and clarify what those choices are. The architect must then frame those choices in a way that will be in the best interest of the entire ecosystem.

Change Team

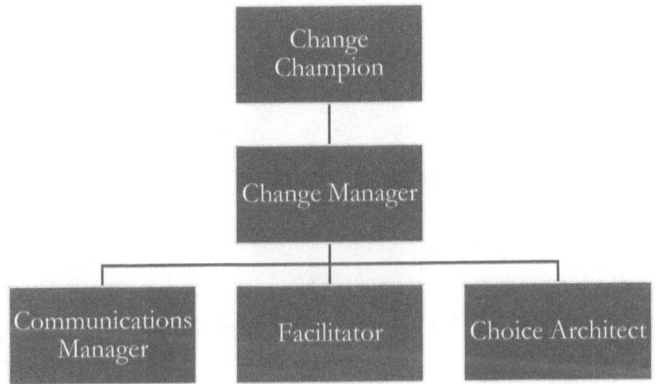

NOTES:

1. What expectations do you have of a change
    champion?

    _____

    _____

    _____

    _____

2. What skillsets are you looking for in a change
    communications manager?

    _____

    _____

    _____

    _____

3. Who in your organization could play the role
    of choice architect and why would they be
    good at it?

    _____

    _____

    _____

    _____

CHAPTER 9
CONCLUSION

"The only way to make sense out of change is to plunge into it, move with it, and join the dance."

Alan W. Watts

Change management has been the main topic in the lexicon of management studies for the past seventy years. The theories of Lewin, Kotter, and Hiatt, to name a few, have led to the advancement of how change is theorized, conceptualized, and executed. Issues with change management are still experienced today as managers know the change models but continue to execute them poorly.

Compounding this issue is the fact that organizations are not engaging their stakeholders in the change process and are instead trying to force change upon their people. Much of this fear is rooted in the fact that to engage stakeholders in the change process would be to cede some control, which would greatly increase the complexity of the change initiative. Proposed is the 9x change management approach, which incorporates the best aspects of the available change theories and provides a methodology of engaging the workforce in the change while controlling complexity.

NOTES:

1. What is an upcoming major change that you could lead?

   _____

   _____

   _____

   _____

2. What in this book would you like to apply and why?

   _____

   _____

   _____

   _____

3. What don't you want to apply from these models?

   _____

   _____

   _____

   _____

REFERENCES

[1] M. Watkins, "Why Daimler Chrysler Never Got Into Gear," *Harvard Business Review,* 2007.

[2] N. Beotra, "Daimler-Chrysler (DCX) Merger: A Cultural Mismatch," 16 October 2016. [Online]. Available: https://medium.com/@beotra.nehaa/daimler-chrysler-dcx-merger-a-cultural-mismatch-2cbb3a05321d.

[3] R. D. Lewis, "Cross-cultural issues relating to the Daimler Chrysler Merge - Case Study," 27 April 2016. [Online]. Available: https://www.crossculture.com/cross-cultural-issues-at-the-daimlerchrysler-merge-case-study/.

[4] C. a. H. Stadler, "Shell, Siemens, and Daimler Chrysler: Leading Change in Companies with

Strong Values," *Long Range Planning,* pp. 1-37, 2005.

[5]   A. a. S. J. D. Cohen, "Daimler Chrysler Merger: The Quest to Create 'One Company'," *Babson College,* pp. 1-26, 2004.

[6]   W. W. Burke, Organizational Change: Theory and Practice, New York: Sage, 2002.

[7]   S. Levine, "What can we learn from the history of change management?," 18 April 2016. [Online]. Available: https://www.cuinsight.com/can-learn-history-change-management.html.

[8]   B. Syed, "The Evolution of Organizational Change Management," 25 November 2015. [Online]. Available: https://www.linkedin.com/pulse/evolution-change-management-burhan-syed-pmp/.

[9]   R. a. F. W. Suddaby, "History and Organizational Change," *Journal of Management,* pp. 19-37, 2017.

[10] C. Brisson-Banks, "Managing Change and Transitions: A Comparison of Different Models and Their Commonalities," *Emerald insights,* pp. 241-252, 2009.

[11] K. Lewin, Field Theory in Social Science, New York, NY: Harper and Row, 1951.

[12] J. P. Kotter, Leading change, Boston, MA: Harvard Business School Press, 1996.

[13] "ADKAR Change Management: creating change in Individuals," 6 November 2018. [Online]. Available: https://www.educational-business-articles.com/adkar-change-management/.

[14] "Organizational Change Models and Their Applications," 6 November 2018. [Online]. Available: https://communicationmgmt.usc.edu/blog/3-organizational-change-models-and-their-applications/.

[15] "What is the ADKAR Model," 6 November 2018. [Online]. Available: https://www.prosci.com/adkar/adkar-model.

[16] S. a. G. O. Ledbetter, "The Nagging Issues of Nudging," 6 November 2018. [Online]. Available: https://medium.com/practical-motivation-science/the-nagging-issues-of-nudging-f0af3a8f8b5.

[17] R. H. &. S. C. R. Thaler, Nudge: Improving decisions about health, wealth, and happiness, New Haven, CN: Yale University Press, 2008.

[18] J. Kotter, "Why Transformation Efforts Fail," *Harvard Management Update,* p. 5, 2005.

9M CONSULTING

About 9m Consulting

9m Consulting helps enable innovation for businesses that are navigating transformation. Unlike other firms, we specialize in building a creative culture that can pivot.

Our Approach

9m is a firm dedicated to guiding organizations through large-scale transitions. Our approach is to work with our clients to understand their issues, opportunities, and perspectives. Instead of applying a one-size-fits-all approach, we apply 9m's agile innovation model. This is more than a process but a framework that provides the right solution to the right problem.

➢ Beginning with culture, 9m diagnoses the current environment and impediments to innovation.
➢ This leads to the next focus area of leadership development and team dynamics. We prime the

teams for group innovation through development and creativity training.

➤ Next, we provide customized, facilitated events that enable creative pinnacles. These events range from strategic planning and business development to problem-solving and product development.

➤ With creation comes disruption. 9m is able to shift its attention to change management planning. We guide clients through a change simulation model to transition the organization expertly. Next, we guide the strategy selection and implementation planning.

<u>9m Approach</u>

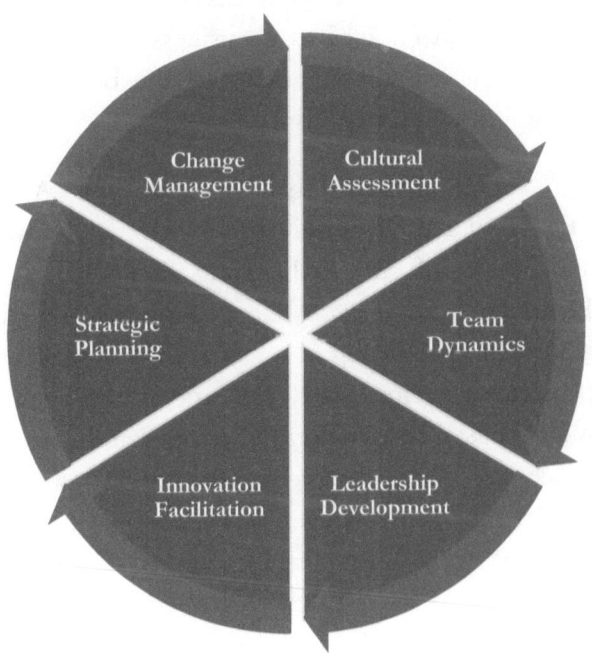

ABOUT THE AUTHOR

Author and Principal Consultant

Matt D.M. Watson, Ph.D., PMP, is the founder and Principal of 9m, an innovation consulting firm based in Boise, Idaho. He began his career in the United States Air Force as a forward-air-controller, serving in the invasion of Iraq with the 101st Airborne Division. Following Matt's service, he worked with the Bechtel Corporation as an organizational development project manager and training director. Later he worked with Hewlett-Packard as a business strategy project manager and is the Chairman of the Board for the Community Veterans Justice Project.

He obtained his Bachelor of Arts in Organizational Leadership from Chapman University and Master of Arts in Learning Technologies from Pepperdine University. After spending the first half of his career specializing in organizational development, project management, and lean process improvements, Matt focused his craft on the creative and innovation processes while completing his Ph.D. in Global Leadership and Change at Pepperdine University. There he was able to refine his innovation model while completing his research on the enablement of creativity.

He is the author of the following:

- ➤ Corporate Musings During the Pandemic
- ➤ The Workplace Olympian
- ➤ Strategy for the Small Business
- ➤ The Strategy Pocketbook: Building a Strategy for Tomorrow's Organization
- ➤ Nudge Change Management: Moving Organizations with Data and Transparency
- ➤ Rethinking Change Management with Nudges: Transforming Organizations in 45 Minutes
- ➤ Facilitating Innovation: Unlocking Moonshots
- ➤ Enabling Innovation: Building a Creative Culture in 45 Minutes
- ➤ The Leadership That Facilitates Innovation
- ➤ From Global Vision to Agile Execution: A Proposed Planning Model
- ➤ Simulating the Corporate Reorganization
- ➤ Common Strategies and Practices Among Facilitators of Innovative Thinking in Organizations
- ➤ Fear and Loathing in the Accountable Culture

www.ingramcontent.com/pod-product-compliance
Lightning Source LLC
Chambersburg PA
CBHW020622220526
45463CB00006B/2653